Corporate Finance Fundamentals

Big Business Theory
for SME, Investor or MBA Application

by Saad

Disclaimer

The material in this publication (the "book") and the information accessed through it is of a general nature only and does not contain investment recommendations or professional advice.

The information is not to be relied upon as being accurate, complete or up to date. Bidi Capital Pty Ltd (the "publisher") recommends that, before acting or not acting upon information contained or referred to in this book, readers should seek independent professional advice that takes into account their financial situation, investment objectives, particular needs and/or other personal circumstances.

The information contained in this book is not to be used for any purpose other than education and it is not to be construed as an indication or prediction of future results from any investment. Bidi Capital Pty Ltd does not offer financial, business or study advice.

To the maximum extent permitted by law, the author and publisher disclaim all responsibility and liability to any person, arising from directly or indirectly from any person taking or not taking action based upon the information in this publication.

"Dedicated to everyone who has affected my life in any way.
Including you…!"

TABLE OF CONTENTS

About accofina, the business behind this book..........................7

Preface..8
   How this book is Meant to be Read? 9

Chapter 1: Risk & Return 11
   1.1 What is Risk & Return?..11
   1.2 Return on Investment 12
   1.3 Residual Income: 14
   1.4 Types of Investment Risks.....................................16
      1.4.1 Systematic Risk 17
      1.4.2 Unsystematic Risk 17
      1.4.3 Credit (or Default) Risk 17
      1.4.4 Foreign Currency Risk 18
      1.4.5 Interest Rate Risk 18
      1.4.6 Political Risk 18
      1.4.7 Market Risk... 18

Chapter 2: Equity VS Debt.. 20
   2.1 Equity Financing 20
      2.1.1 Common Stock.. 21
      2.1.2 Preferred Stock.. 23
      2.1.3 Convertible Preferred Stock 25
   2.2 Debt Financing..25
      2.2.1 Income Bonds 26
      2.2.2 Mortgage Bonds 26
      2.2.3 Subordinated Debentures and Second Mortgage bonds. 26
      2.2.4 First Mortgage Bonds 27
      2.2.5 US Treasury Bonds 27
   2.3 Asset Valuation...28
      2.3.1 Capital Asset Pricing Model (CAPM) 28

Chapter 3: Bonds 31
   3.1 What are bonds? 31
   3.2 Amortization of Interest......................................33
   3.3 Why Bother With Bonds Anyway?.......................35
   3.4 Bonds Issued at Premium or Discount....................37
   3.5 How a Bond's Discount or Premium is dealt with?.............39

3.6 Amortization of Discount or Premium over the term of a Bond 41

3.7 How Bonds are Differentiated 43

   3.7.1 Maturity Pattern.. 44

   3.7.2 Valuation... 44

   3.7.3 Redemption Provisions 44

   3.7.4 Securitization 45

   3.7.5 Ownership.. 45

   3.7.6 Priority 46

   3.7.7 Repayment Provisions 46

3.8 How the Bonds risks are analyzed?......................... 46

Chapter 4: Capital Structure of a Business 48

4.1 Cost of Capital 48

4.2 Components of Cost of Capital................................. 49

   4.2.1 Cost of Long Term Debt (LTD) 50

   4.2.2 Cost of Preferred and Common Stock (Cost of Equity - COE)... 50

4.3 Weighted Average Cost of Capital (WACC)............ 52

4.4 Optimal Capital Structure 53

4.5 Marginal Cost of Capital (MCC) 55

Chapter 5: Capital Budgeting.................................... 56

5.1 Relevant Cash Flows 56

5.2 Net Present Value (NPV) 57

5.3 Internal Rate of Return (IRR) 60

5.4 Payback Period 61

   5.4.1 Upsides of Payback Period................................. 63

   5.4.2 Downsides of Payback Period 63

5.5 Accounting Rate of Return 63

   5.5.1 Upsides of ARR 64

   5.5.2 Downsides of ARR.. 65

5.6 Economic Value Added 65

Chapter 6: Cash Management & Working Capital............ 67

6.1 Why should the firm maintain a minimum balance of idle funds?... 67

6.2 Compensating Balance 68

6.3 Speeding up Cash Collections & Slowing Cash Disbursements 69

   6.3.1 The Float.. 69

6.3.2 Offering Discounts... 69
6.3.3 Factoring Receivables... 70
6.3.4 Lock Box System 71
6.3.5 Draft... 71
6.3.6 Payable through Draft (PTD) 72
6.3.7 Zero Balance Account (ZBA) 72
6.3.8 Disbursement Float... 73
6.4 Spontaneous Financing...73
6.5 To Take or Not To Take a Discount? 74
6.6 Short Term Financing Arrangements. 75
6.7 Effective Interest Rate...76
6.8 Loans with a Compensating Balance 79
6.9 Secured Financing:..81
6.10 Chapter Conclusion...82

Chapter 7: Managing Your Risks 84
7.1 Basics of Risk Management...84
7.1.1 Risk Acceptance 84
7.1.2 Risk Avoidance 85
7.1.3 Risk Reduction 85
7.1.4 Risk Sharing... 85
7.2 Derivatives...86
7.3 Hedging 86
7.3.1 Options.. 88
7.3.2 Forward Contract 91
7.3.3 Futures Contract.. 93
7.4 Chapter Conclusion...93

Summary 94

Extras 101
Book Excerpt.. 101
Free accofina.com Resources.. 105
More Books and Other accofina Products 107
accofina Contact Details and Review Request............................ 109

About accofina, the business behind this book

accofina is the publisher of, and the business behind, this book.

After earlier iterations, **accofina.com** was launched in August 2013 and is a hub for accounting & finance education and technology products.

On the website you will find books, iOS apps, online courses & tutorials, MS Excel spreadsheets and other online calculators all customized to assist putting academic accounting & finance knowledge, through various technology platforms, in the hands of businesspeople, investors and students.

accofina is part of Bidi Capital Pty Ltd, a company registered in NSW Australia.

Preface

Ever wonder why the big giants of the corporate world have an army of financial analysts at their disposal, monitoring each and every investment opportunity?

Being a conglomerate, they have all the access to the resources to finance their strategic objectives and still they dedicate a huge portion of their wealth in getting their heads around the fact about which financial option to choose?

In fact, if they are such profitable ventures, then why even bother about what financing mode to opt for? Just use your profits and invest it back in the company and keep everything simple. Right...?

In this book, we will touch topics related to finance and investment from the perspective of the Small and Medium Enterprises (SMEs) that unlike the big guns don't have access to the large pool of talent of Corporate Strategy Makers, Financial Analysts and Chartered Accountants etc.

SMEs usually run tight on money so it becomes even more paramount to manage their funds effectively and efficiently by making sure that only the option with a great balance of risk and return is chosen.

After reading this book you will be able to analyze different investment opportunities in terms of:

- Relative risk and return.
- Different modes of financing.
- How to calculate the cost of capital.

- How to evaluate the profitability of different investments.
- How and where to perfectly utilize your extra money.
- How to manage risks that revolve around your investments.

We will explain all terminology in order to make sure that our readers grasp each and every concept that is necessary to understand this book. However, assuming that our average reader is aware of the basic accounting treatments and jargon, we will not go through explaining the accounting concepts in great detail.

Having said that, this book is perfect for those who are running their own businesses (especially SMEs) but face difficulty in understanding the concept of financial management and find it too complex to play around with and thus make use of their extra funds.

Additionally, students looking for a quick reference to understand the basic financial management concepts can also benefit from this book.

If you do want to understand a bit more of fundamental accounting, you can access a free eBook, "Accounting: Foundation Inputs & Outputs" via this link: **http://www.accofina.com/accounting-foundations.html**

How this book is Meant to be Read?

We have tried our best to make this book an easy read by explaining all topics in the most conversational and friendly tone available, avoided use of unnecessary technical jargon (without explaining them) and have made sure to give an example for every relevant topic.

We would suggest our readers to read this book from two perspectives.

The first is from the perspective of an investor (lender) who is looking to invest his or her idle cash or hard earned money in some profitable venture. Read every topic as if you want to skeptically analyze each and every prospect before you hand over your money to someone. Being aware of the intricacies involved in any sound investment decision will help you a lot and help you grow your business.

The second perspective we would suggest you is that of a borrower or prospective investment, a person who needs to convince others to invest in their idea. We all are aware of the fact that owning your business is a bumpy ride and sometimes you just need to reach out to others in particular situations and raise capital.

In such cases, beforehand knowledge of how you are going to raise finance and what sources of finances are actually available for you will really help you in cutting an optimum deal and will enable you to raise maximum finance with minimum risk.

Before we start this book, we wish you a good luck and hope that this book will prove helpful for you to excel in your entrepreneurial endeavors.

Chapter 1: Risk & Return

1.1 What is Risk & Return?

You must be aware of these two terms. At their very basics, risk and return can be defined as:

Risk: *The condition of uncertainty that anything can go wrong.*

Return: *The compensation that an investor receives for undergoing the condition of Risk.*

Once you understand these definitions clearly, it becomes quite intuitive that the greater the odds that something can go wrong (high risk), the greater will be the compensation (high return). Or in very simple words:

Higher risk calls for higher return.

Obviously, a rational investor would never invest in a much riskier investment if he or she were sure that the same amount of return could be achieved by investing in different opportunity that is less risky than the former, and thus one would demand higher return on investment opportunities inheriting higher risks.

Like the famous concept of "Supply and Demand" in Economics, the rule of "Risk and Return" forms the basis of financial management and all the decisions related to investments are boiled down to these two basic factors.

After getting hold of the concept of Risk and Return, let's see

how we normally apply the concept of "Return" in our daily

business lives.

1.2 Return on Investment

The foremost and primary criteria used by the investors in ascertaining the strength of their investments is by gauging the Return on Investment (ROI).

There is no rocket science behind this. It's simply the measure of the return in excess of your investment (if calculated with an absolute amount) or the efficiency of your investment (if calculated with a percentage).

ROI (with absolute terms)
= Gain on Investment – Cost of Investment

ROI (with a percentage)
= (Gain on Investment – Cost of Investment) / Cost of Investment

You can calculate your ROI in any of the two ways: In absolute terms or with a percentage.

What method you use depends on what you want to measure. If you want to measure just the return that you generate above your investment then ROI (in absolute terms) will be sufficient for you. However, if you want to compare different investment opportunities, then you should be looking at using a percentage.

Here's a simple example to understand this.

Example:

Let's suppose that you plan to sell apples. For that, you will have to first buy them and that will cost you US $100. That will be your investment.

Now, you manage to sell those apples for US $120. Hence, your ROI in amount will be:

ROI (absolute) = $120 - $100

ROI (absolute) = $20

Simple. Isn't it?

However, when you don't have any other opportunity to invest in then ROI (absolute) will be suitable for you. But when it comes to comparing different opportunities, this method has its limitations that can be understood from the example below:

Example:

Continuing above example, let's suppose that now you have two investment opportunities. Either to sell apple or oranges. Oranges cost US $150 and would sell at US $175.

If you see the amount, it's quite apparent that it's much more profitable to sell oranges as it will generate you an ROI of ($175 - $150 = $25) which is US $5 more than selling apples.

However, if you analyze the percentage return, you will get a totally different picture:

ROI for Apples (%) = ($120 - $100) / $100

ROI for Apples (%) = 20%

ROI for Oranges (%) = ($175 - $150) / $100

ROI for Oranges (%) = 16.67%

It's quite evident that investing in apples is more efficient than investing in oranges when it comes to assessing the percentage return on your investment as compared to when you measure the returns in terms of an absolute amount.

So deciding which method to use depends on what you want to achieve. As a general rule of thumb, calculating the percentage return is much more desirable when comparing two or more investment opportunities.

However, the major drawback of this method is that it does not account for the risk.

Quite possibly, there may be a much greater chance of people tastes changing and they will not buy apples anymore.

So, when it comes to assessing investment options in terms of risks, ROI does not prove to be your best friend.

We will discuss the effects of risk on return later. First, let's have a look at the very basic concept of **Residual Income**.

1.3 Residual Income:

The above example of calculating ROI is fairly simple one. In the real world and more sophisticated environments, your cost of doing and running a business is much more complicated and encompasses even more elements than just the cost of acquiring the material to sell it, like the apples and oranges we discussed above.

In order to reach a much more refined decision, it is necessary to appreciate all of these other costs as well.
Residual Income is the income that an individual or a business earns above its target return that is set before investing the capital.

Target return is the minimum return that one is expecting from a project.

Residual Income can be calculated as follows:

> *Residual Income*
> *= Operating Income – Target Return on Invested Capital*

With residual income, decision-making becomes relatively simpler when deciding whether to accept a project or not.

a. *If the Residual Income is positive then the project should be accepted.*
b. *If the Residual Income is negative then the project should be rejected.*

Example:

A person decides to invest in an opportunity demanding initial investment of US $10,000. The investment is able to generate US $13,500 operating income.

The target return set by the person is at least US $14,000.

If the Residual Income method is chosen in order to evaluate the opportunity, the person's decision would be:

> *Residual Income = $13,500 - $14,000*
>
> *= ($500)*

Since the residual income of the project is negative $500, despite being profitable, the project should be Rejected.

The biggest advantage of using residual income is its decisiveness. You can decide if the project is worth undertaking without going into much detail.

Additionally, since it ensures that only those investments to be made will guarantee a return above a target threshold, the residual income method is more consistent with profit maximization.

What this means is that when making multiple investments, investors usually get carried away with focusing on just profits so much so that they forget that a particular project, despite being profitable might be decreasing the aggregate return of all the other investments. In other words, it's not just about making profitable investments, it's about the MOST (or best) profitable investments between a number of choices.

In the example above, an investment was declined despite being profitable because the investor projected that his overall return would decrease as other projects might be generating more return.

As we have discussed the basic notion of return and we have figured out that using only the return on your investment does not give you the whole picture, one must see the bigger picture and evaluate on the basis of the risks that he is undertaking.

Therefore, appreciation of different types of risks is mandatory.

1.4 Types of Investment Risks

Broadly speaking, risk can be divided into following two major categories:

- **Systematic Risk.**

- **Unsystematic Risk.**

1.4.1 Systematic Risk

Often called as "Non-Diversifiable Risk", this is the risk of collapse of the whole system instead of any particular segment/sector.

For example: the Financial Crisis of 2008.

As the risk cannot be associated with any one segment of the industry, it is almost virtually impossible to prevent it by diversifying your investment.

1.4.2 Unsystematic Risk

Also known as "specific risk", "unique risk" or "diversifiable risk" it is the risk of the collapse of a particular segment of industry.

For example: the downfall of telegrams after the advent of telephones.

The above categories of risk can be further divided into the following sub-categories:

1.4.3 Credit (or Default) Risk

The risk that the borrower will eventually default and won't be able to pay their debts.

1.4.4 Foreign Currency Risk

The risk that the movement of currency exchange rates will result in unfavorable changes in your wealth.

For example: As a result of depreciation of British Pound, your investment in the UK is now worth less than it was before the movement.

1.4.5 Interest Rate Risk

The risks that interest rate movements will eventually make you pay higher interest on your borrowing or earn you lower interest on your investments.

1.4.6 Political Risk

The risk that a country's government will change their policies in a way not favorable to your business.

1.4.7 Market Risk

This is the most popular and widely discussed form of risk and generally speaking, it means that the market will not perform according to your expectations hence causing your overall wealth or return to decline.

Having mentioned all the possible types of risks, it should be kept in mind that if on one hand the "Return" can be measured objectively, for e.g. 20% return on investment, the evaluation of risk is more of a subjective matter.

Efforts are being made to bring the risk under the realm of objectivity by conceiving different types of Risk Models, but still, the identification of risk on an objective basis stays a hot topic of debate among entrepreneurs and business analysts and the only best way to reach to any conclusion about the magnitude of risk depends a lot on one's experience and business acumen.

Chapter 2: Equity VS Debt

The inherent risks in different financing options available affects your choice between the alternatives and you prioritize what mode to opt for to raise additional finance or to make investments based on your risk analysis.

Before explaining further, it is necessary to understand the two major ways in which a business can raise finance. These are:

2.1 Equity Financing

Equity Financing is a method of finance in which a firm surrenders its ownership interest (or part ownership) in return for a monetary value. The ownership surrendered is normally considered to be worth the consideration received against it.

In equity financing, the financiers (normally called shareholders) are not assured regular payments in return for their investment and are considered the last to be compensated, in the case of the firm going broke (liquidation), from the residual funds when financiers are being compensated in this process.

Hence, equity financing is deemed to be more costly because the shareholders demand greater return against the higher risk that they are willing to take in the form of uncertainty of regular payments.

Moreover, in order to convince possible investors, a compensatory factor that shareholders are provided with is the possibility of greater returns in form of dividends or profit distribution when the business performs well, in relation to the return of other forms of finance.

Due to some obvious and quite explicit reasons, there is a general consensus about the perceived risks and potential returns of some of the investments/securities:

Nature	Instrument	Risk and Return
Equity	Common Stock Convertible preferred stock Preferred stock	Highest
Debt	Income Bonds Subordinated debentures Second mortgage bonds First mortgage bonds U.S. Treasury bonds	Lowest

Brief explanations of each of the equity and debt instruments mentioned above are as follow:

2.1.1 Common Stock

These are the normal shareholders of the company. Being equity ownership in nature, they are considered to be the most risky investments, as the return is not guaranteed a return and are last in priority when a business liquidates.

a. **Advantages to the Issuer**
   1. Since the dividends are not fixed, they are paid from the profits when available.
   2. No fixed maturity date.

b. Disadvantages to the Issuer

1. When new common stocks are issued, they dilute the control of the existing shareholders.
2. Underwriting costs (i.e. the cost the issuer has to bear when issuing common stocks)
3. Cash dividends on common stocks are not tax-deductible which means that they must be paid out after tax profits.

2.1.1.1 How the Common Stocks are Valued?

There are two methods used for common stock valuation:

a. When the dividend per share is constant and is expected to be paid continuously. In this case, the price per share is calculated as:

$$P_0 = D \div r$$

Where:

P_0 = current price per share
D = Dividend per share
r = required rate of return

b. When the dividend is assumed to grow at the constant rate. It is also known as Dividend Discount Model. The price per share in this model is calculated as:

$$P_0 = D_0 (1 + g) \div (r - g)$$

Where:

P_0 = *current price per share*
D_0 = *current dividend per share*
D_1 = *dividend per share expected next year*
r = *required rate of return (cost of common stock)*
g = *growth rate*

Example:

A company just announced and paid a dividend of $1 per share. The dividend is expected to grow at a constant rate of 5% per year and investor's required rate of return is 6%. Market value of the company's share is:

$$P_0 = D_0 (1 + g) \div (r - g)$$

$$= \$1(1 + 5\%) \div (6\% - 5\%)$$

$$= 1.05 \div 0.01$$

$$= \$105 \text{ per share}$$

2.1.2 Preferred Stock

Preferred stocks have features of both debt and equity despite being equity in nature. They have a fixed payments but the issuer is not obliged to pay dividends. Generally, they also lack the voting rights that are enjoyed by the common stockholders. However, some classes of preferred stock may also have voting rights as well.

In case of liquidation, preferred shareholders have priority over common shareholders but will be subordinate when it comes to paying the debt holders.

In case of cumulative preference shares, the dividend keeps

getting accumulated every year and the issuer is bound to pay dividends in case of residual profits.

a. **Advantages to the Issuer**
   1. *Preferred shares are a form of equity finance and therefore increase the creditworthiness of the entity.*
   2. *Control still remains in the hands of the common shareholders.*
   3. *Failure to pay dividends will not lead to bankruptcy, as periodic payments are not mandatory to preferred shareholders.*

b. **Disadvantages to the Issuer**
   1. *Cash dividends paid are not tax deductible therefore tax is paid before the dividends are paid to the preferred shareholders.*

2.1.2.1 How preferred stocks are valued?

Just like common stocks, the value of preferred stock is also dependent on the return expected from them. This return is the dividend.

$$P_0 = D_p \div r$$

Where:

P_0 = *current share price*
D_p = *dividend per share*
r = *required rate of return*

Example:

A class of preferred share with a par value of $150, dividend rate of

6% and a required rate of return by the investors of 5% will have a market value of:

$$P_0 = D_p \div r$$
$$= (\$150 \times 6\%) \div 5\%$$
$$= \$9 \div 5\%$$
$$= \$180 \text{ per share}$$

2.1.3 Convertible Preferred Stock

Convertible preferred stocks are issued as preferred stock initially but they have an option of being converted to common stock at maturity.

They are riskier than preferred stocks because of being converted into common stock later in the period but less risky than common stocks because of enjoying the privileges of preferred stock as well.

2.2 Debt Financing

Debt financing is the normal case of lending and borrowing in which a lender issues funds to the borrower against a commitment of series of regular or one off payment any time later in the future.

In case of dissolution (and liquidation), the lenders of debt are given priority rights from the funds of the business and are compensated before the equity financiers.

Since the payments are guaranteed, debt financing is considered to be cheaper (for the borrower, because payments are bound and thus have less risk to the lender) than the equity financing.

One way of raising debt finance is through bonds.

2.2.1 Income Bonds

Income bonds pay interest contingent on the issuer's profitability. Since the return on these bonds depends heavily on the financial position of the issuer, they hold higher risks as compared to any other class of bonds.

2.2.2 Mortgage Bonds

These bonds are backed by specific assets which are used a compensation in case the issuer fails to pay the lender. The proceeds from the sale of the asset are then used to compensate the lender. Since the payments are guaranteed in form of the assets (often referred to as **collateral**), mortgage bonds bear less risk as compared to the equity finance and income bonds.

2.2.3 Subordinated Debentures and Second Mortgage bonds

Because of the certain terms and conditions in the **indenture** (the contract outlining the terms of the bond), these types of bonds hold inferior claims on the entity's assets as compared to other senior bonds.
Second Mortgage Bonds are actually secondary claim to an original mortgage bond. In other words, it is actually a bond issued on a mortgage.

In the event of liquidation, the original mortgage receives the funds from the liquidation of the collateral until those bonds are fully paid off.

Since they have secondary claim, they are perceived to be more risky than their counterparts that enjoy the privilege of primary claim and thus these bonds are more costly to raise.

2.2.4 First Mortgage Bonds

First mortgage bonds are bonds secured by an underlying asset (collateral) having real value like land, building etc.

In the event of default, the bondholders have a claim over that property which they have right to sell in order to compensate for their loss.

2.2.5 US Treasury Bonds

These are marketable bonds offered by the Government of US. Often referred to as T-bonds, they offer fixed interest rates and generally last for 10 years.

Since they have a credibility of a state behind them, they are considered to be the trust worthiest, as a state is least likely to ever default (unless it's Greece).

Therefore, when it comes to the risk and return, US Treasury Bonds, being the least risky investments to invest in, also offer the lowest return comparable to every other security.

Hence, the return on T-bonds can be set as a benchmark where every other security should yield more than US Treasury Bonds.

As you now know the basic instruments of equity and debts,

let's have a look at what return to expect from equity investments based on their level of risks. This evaluation is normally known as Capital Asset Pricing Model (CAPM).

2.3 Asset Valuation

2.3.1 Capital Asset Pricing Model (CAPM)

The Capital Asset Pricing Model (CAPM) quantifies the expected return from equity instruments based on their level of risks and compares them with the average level of return available in the market.

CAPM follows the idea that the investor must be compensated for his investment in two ways: For the 'time value of money' and for the risk he/she has undertaken.

As we know, generally the most risky investment is someone investing in the common stock and, at the other end of the spectrum, U.S Treasury bonds are the least risky instruments. CAPM also seems to appreciating this fact.

The formula for CAPM is:

$$\text{Required Rate of Return} = R_f + \beta\,(R_m - R_f)$$

Where:
* R_f = *Risk free rate of return (This is the return provided by the safest investments, e.g. the U.S Treasury bonds in our case)*
* R_m = *Market Return*
* β *(beta)* = *Measure of the systematic risk or the volatility of the individual security in comparison to the market.*

I.   *The equation, $(R_m - R_f)$ is also known as Market Risk Premium, which is the premium returned by the market above the risk free rate.*

II. *The effect of the individual security over the volatility of the portfolio is measured by its sensitivity to movements by the overall market. This sensitivity is stated in terms of beta (β) coefficient.*

III. *Thus the beta of market portfolio is supposed to be 1 and the beta coefficient of U.S Treasury bonds is considered 0.*

Example:

An investor considering the purchase of a stock with a beta value of 1.1. Treasury bills are currently paying 9.2% and the average return of the market is 10.5%. What is the return that the normal investor will be expecting from this investment?

Here:

$\beta = 1.1$
$Rf = 9.2\%$
$Rm = 10.5\%$

Required Rate of Return $= Rf + \beta \ (Rm - Rf)$

$= 9.2\% + 1.1 \ (10.5\% - 9.2\%)$
$= 9.2\% + 1.43\%$
$= 10.63\%$

With the stated level of risk, a rational investor should be looking forward to earn 10.63% in returns for this particular investment with the above-mentioned details.

This chapter has dealt with the basics of financing and different types of finance that are available to a common investor and businessperson. However, the million-dollar question that businesspeople are always trying to keep figuring out is: what should be the appropriate combination of the debt and equity in any business.

We will deal with the nitty gritty of appropriate capital structure (combination of debt and equity) the later in the book but first, let's dive into more details about bonds in the next chapter.

Chapter 3: Bonds

3.1 What are bonds?

Bonds are form of long term debt financing for corporations and government entities. We used the terms corporations and government entities because issuing bonds requires the financial credibility that is usually only enjoyed by these entities.

Bonds are a formal contractual obligation to pay an amount of money (called the par value, maturity amount or face amount) to the holder at a certain date.

In addition to the par value, a series of cash interest payments, based on a predetermined percentage, are also paid. This is called the coupon rate and normally applies on the face amount of the bond.

There are two logical arguments for demanding interest on lending.

The first is that when the lender gives away his or her money they are actually helping out the borrower temporarily. So in return for this help they demand interest on their lending as a form of service charge. This rationale normally works for short-term borrowings.

The second logic is that when a creditor gives away his or her money for a longer period of time, say 10 years, their money loses its value over the period of time that is highly proportional to the inflation incurred over the years. This means that one million US dollars will not be worth the same value 10 years later.

So, interest is a way to get compensated for the loss of value over a period of time. We will learn about the time value of money later in this book but in order to understand the concept of the second logic of interest, read the example below:

Example:

Suppose a person lends you his money (US $1) for 5 years. The inflation rate is expected to be 10% (average) over the term of 5 years. This means that every dollar will be worth 10% less than the last year or, in other words, every year any commodity that was US $1 last year will now cost 10% more than the last year. Therefore, after first year, the price of any item of US $1 will be:

Year	Price before inflation	Inflation	Price after inflation
0	1	-	1
1	1	10%	1.1
2	1.1	10%	1.21
3	1.21	10%	1.33
4	1.33	10%	1.46
5	1.46	10%	1.61

According to the projection, US $1 today will have a value of US $1.61 after 5 years. So paying back just $1 after 5 years to the lender will not do justice and therefore, additional $0.61 needs to be paid as well so as to compensate for the loss of value.

This $0.61 is the interest.

This also means that having money now is worth more beneficial than having the same amount of money later.

3.2 Amortization of Interest

In the above example, we have tried not to complicate things and have taken just US $1 dollar as an amount borrowed. However, in reality the actual amounts are much greater than this and therefore, the interest payable on them as well.
It would be too burdensome if the borrower were required to pay all of the interest in just one go. Therefore, the interest payments are spread over the total term of the borrowing along with the principal payment.

This spreading of interest over the term of the borrowing is called *amortization* of interest.

Example:

Continuing above example, where we calculated that total interest payable over the 5 years on US $1 with an inflation rate of 10% is $0.61. Dividing it over 5 years we will have:

Interest payable every   =   *$0.61 ÷ 5 years*
         year

                 $0.12 per year

Hence, in order to pay back a loan of US $1 in 5 years along with the principal amount, the borrower will have to pay:

Principal amount per year   =   *$1 ÷ 5 years*

                     =   *$0.2 per year*

$$\text{Total amount payable per year} \quad = \quad \textit{principal + interest}$$

$$= \quad \$0.2 + \$0.12$$

$$= \quad \$0.32 \textit{ per year}$$

So, with an annual payment of $0.32, which includes principal and interest portion, the borrower will be able to pay off his loan and the investor will get his money back along with the compensation of the loss of value that his funds have to face.

All the terms that include details about regular payments to the total term of the loan arrangement are decided between both parties and are stated in the form of written agreement is called **indenture**.

Generally, the longer the bond takes to mature, the higher its coupon rate will be. Since the risk of interest rate fluctuations is greater in the long run, the investors demand higher compensation in return for exposing themselves to these longer-term risks.

This relationship of interest rate and time to maturity of bonds can be depicted in the following graph also known as yield curve.

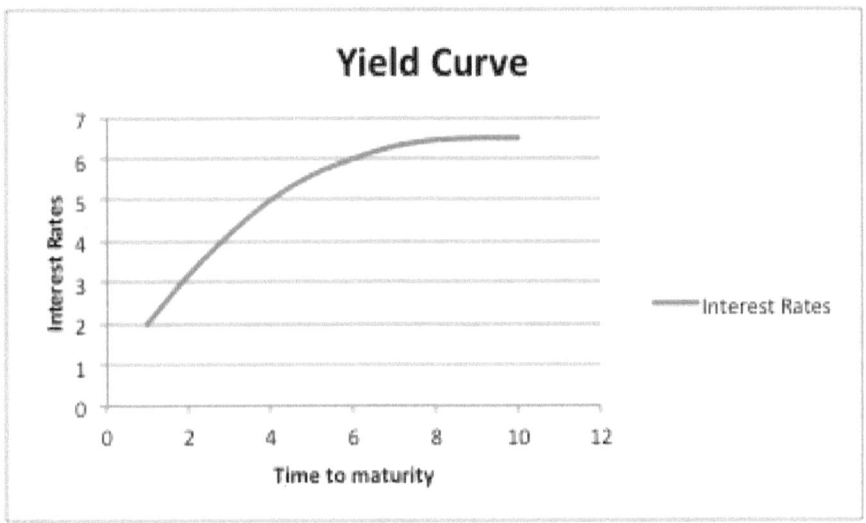

The series of regular payments made by the borrower at a specified frequency to payback the amount borrowed through bonds are called annuities.

The most common payment frequencies are monthly, quarterly, semi-annually and yearly.

There are two basic types of annuities:

i. **Ordinary Annuity:** When the payments are made at the end of each period.
ii. **Annuity Due:** When the payments are made at the beginning of each period.

3.3 Why Bother With Bonds Anyway?

In order to understand the significance of bonds, let us tell you how bonds work.

A borrower goes out and asks for some funds. A lender, who

has sufficient money to lend out, evaluates this investment opportunity and sees bonds as a source of regular income, since he's being paid regular interest payments along with the portion of the principal on his amount.

The terms of bonds are described somewhat in the following manner:

100 $1,000 10 years bonds with coupon rate of 8%.

Generally this means that:
- *The total par (or market) value of the bond is, 100 x $1,000 = $100,000*
- *The bond will mature in 10 years.*
- *Total interest payable by the borrower is: $100,000 x 8% = $8,000*

The interest payments on the bonds are based on the terms agreed by both parties. This can be annually, semi-annually, quarterly or monthly.

The interest rate on bonds is often quoted as ***coupon rate***.

This is the simplest explanation of the bond's terms. In the example above, the par value of the bonds have been stated as $1,000 per bond, and thus, it seems quite obvious that whoever is going to buy these bonds will have to pay $1,000 for each bond.

However, when it comes to real world, the arrangement is little bit more complex than what has been mentioned here and the par value of bonds tend to keep fluctuating due to various reasons.

One of these reasons being the interest rates offered by the market, in general, on similar instruments (that have the same nature).

Needless to say that when the interest rates offered by the market on the similar instrument tends to increase, as compared with the interest offered by the bonds, the bond loses its value as the investors now have more lucrative opportunity to invest into.

Quite opposite is the case when the market interest rates tend to fall in relation to those offered by the bond.

To appreciate the fluctuating interest rates in the market, the borrowers keep changing the par value of the bonds in order to keep the interest of the lenders intact within their instrument.

The movement of the value of the bonds and offering it to the lenders either below or above their market rates is called issuing bonds at discount or premium respectively.

3.4 Bonds Issued at Premium or Discount

*When bonds are issued at price lower than their market value, then they are **issued at discount.***

*When bonds are issued at price higher than their market value, then they are **issued at premium.***

Though the interest rate is the major factor in deciding the market values of the bonds, it is not the only feature of the bond that decides the bond's market value.

In fact, to reach any agreement with the bond's fair value, one has to look into many other elements as well which include the risk associated with the bond, the financial condition of the borrower, etc.

One important aspect to understand about the bonds being issued less than or greater than their par value is that no matter what their issued value is, the bonds are considered to mature, and interest payments are made, at their par value.

Sounds confusing? Don't worry. Have a look at this small example.

Example:

Let's say that a bond with a par value of $1,000, with a coupon rate of 5% and a maturity date of 5 years from now is issued at a discount of $100. Hence its issued value is $900.

However, the interest paid will be on the original par value, which is $1,000 instead of its issued value of $900.

Similarly, the borrower will assume that the lender has provided with an amount $1,000 instead of $900 and will have to pay him $1,000 at the bond's maturity.

The case is the same with bonds issued at premium. The par value will have prevalence when it comes to the interest payments and the amount to be paid back at the time of maturity.

The issued value is just to entice lenders from the perspective of discounted bonds or to take advantage of the different interest rates being offered when issuing at the premium.

Having said that, how does one treat this discount and premium?
The simple answer is through amortization of the discount or premium over the term of the bond.

Hopefully you have gotten hold of the concept of amortization

---

above when we discussed it in the case of interest. If not, then we will suggest you to read it again and then come back to this portion of the book.

3.5 How a Bond's Discount or Premium is dealt with?

The simplest answer to this question apart from amortizing it over the bond's life is by increasing and decreasing the amount of interest expense on the books.

Let's have a look at the example below in order to grasp this concept even more firmly.

Example:

At the beginning of the year, a company issues 100 5-years, $10,000 bonds. The market interest rate on the same instrument is either 6% or 10%. However, the interest rate offered by the company is 8%.

Total face value of the bonds is (100 x $10,000) $1,000,000 and the interest payable on 8% is:

$$\$1,000,000 \times 8\% = \$80,000$$

In our case, the maturity period of bond is 5 years and therefore, the annuity factors at 6% and 10% respectively are:

	At 6%	At 10%
Present Value of '1' for 5 periods	0.747	0.621
Present Value of ordinary annuity of '1' for 5 periods	4.212	3.791

* An Annuity factor is the factor at which the value of 1 unit money declines over a period. Read more about devaluation of money in chapter 5 (Section 5.2).

1. *When the bonds stated rate is 8% and the market's interest rates is 6%*

PV of face amount after 5 years [(100 x $10,000) x 0.747] =	$747,000
PV of cash interest paid over 5 years ($80,000 x 4.212) =	$336,960
Cash proceeds from bond issue =	$1,083,960
Par value of bonds =	1,000,000
Amount of premium =	$83,960

2. *When the bonds stated rate is 8% and the market's interest rate is 10%*

PV of face amount after 5 years [(100 x $10,000) x 0.621] =	*$621,000*
PV of cash interest paid over 5 years ($80,000 x 3.791) =	*$303,280*
Cash proceeds from bond issue =	*924,280*
Par value of bonds =	*1,000,000*
Amount of discount =	*$75,720*

3.6 Amortization of Discount or Premium over the term of a Bond

As said above, all the discount or premium on the bonds issued is supposed to be amortized over the term of the bond. In our case, this is 5 years. So the premium of $83,960 and a discount of $75,720 will be amortized over 5 years.

This amortization is done using the **effective-interest method**.

Since the premium or discount does not have any effect on the par value and the actual interest paid on the bond, the amount that is subject to amortization is adjusted in the interest expense within the books.

We will explain this concept further but first, let us have a look at the annual interest expense figure that can be calculated by:

Annual Interest Expense =
Carrying amount of bond at the beginning of the period x Effective interest rate

This interest expense calculated above includes the effects of amortization of discount or premium.

This effect is calculated in the following way:
1. *When the bonds are issued at discount, annual interest expense equals cash interest paid plus the amount of discount amortized*
2. *When the bonds are issued at premium, the annual interest expense equals cash interest paid minus the amount of premium amortized.*

Therefore, in case of discount, your annual interest decreases gradually and increase on annual basis in case of a premium.

If this is turning out to be too complicated, then don't worry. There's always an example to work it out (on the following page).

In case of premium:

Year	Beginning Carrying Amount of Bonds A	Market Interest Rate		Interest Expense		Cash Interest Paid	Premium Amortized B	Remaining Premium	Ending Carrying Amount of Bonds A-B
1	1,083,960	6%	=	65,038	-	80,000	$14,962	$68,998	$1,068,998
2	1,068,998	6%	=	64,140	-	80,000	$15,860	$53,138	$1,053,138
3	1,053,138	6%	=	63,188	-	80,000	$16,812	$36,326	$1,036,326
4	1,036,326	6%	=	62,180	-	80,000	$17,820	$18,506	$1,018,506

In case of discount:

Year	Beginning Carrying Amount of Bonds A	Market Interest Rate		Interest Expense		Cash Interest Paid	Premium Amortized B	Remaining Discount	Ending Carrying Amount of Bonds A+B
1	924,280	10%	=	$92,428	-	80,000	$12,428	$63,292	$936,708
2	936,708	10%	=	$93,671	-	80,000	$13,671	$49,621	$950,379
3	950,379	10%	=	$95,038	-	80,000	$15,038	$34,583	$984,962
4	$984,962	10%	=	$98,496	-	80,000	$18,496	$16,087	$1,003,458

At the maturity date, the premium or discount will be fully amortized *and the carrying value of the bonds will be equal to the face amount.*

3.7 How Bonds are Differentiated

In the last chapter, we discussed the different types of bonds. Let's have a look that how these bonds are classified

.

The bonds are differentiated on the basis of their:
   a. *Maturity Pattern*
   b. *Valuation*

c. *Redemption provisions*
d. *Securitization*
e. *Ownership*
f. *Priority*
g. *Repayment Provisions*

3.7.1 Maturity Pattern

Bonds differentiated on the basis of their maturity pattern are:

a. **Term Bond:** *Bonds with single maturity date which is normally at the end of their terms*
b. **Serial Bond:** *Bonds that mature at regular intervals*

3.7.2 Valuation

a. **Variable Rate Bonds** pay interest that is dependent on the market conditions. They are also known as Floating Rate Bonds.
b. **Zero Coupon Bonds** involve no periodic interest payments. Their interest component is entirely the discounted portion (more on the bonds issued on discount or premium later). They are also called **Deep Discount Bonds** because of the heavy discount on which these bonds are issued.
c. **Commodity Backed Bonds** require payment to be made based on any commodity such as gold.

3.7.3 Redemption Provisions

a. **Callable Bonds** are purchased (or called) by the issuer before their maturity at a specified price. Issuers normally do this during the period of falling interest rates so that the bonds with high interest rates are replaced with lower interest rates bonds.
b. **Convertible Bonds** are converted into equity instruments under certain conditions. Normally the holder of the bonds has the option to opt for the conversion. Since there is a chance of becoming equity holder of a company and have direct share of the profits, normally this works as an inducement for the investors.

3.7.4 Securitization

a. **Mortgage Bonds** are backed by specific assets, usually known as collateral. This asset can be any real asset with an intrinsic value for e.g. land or building etc.
b. **Debentures** are backed by borrower's general credit but not by a specific asset.

3.7.5 Ownership

a. **Registered Bonds** are issued in the name of the holder who is entitled to receive the interest and principal payments.
b. **Bearer Bonds** are totally opposite of the registered bonds. They are not registered in the name of any particular holder. Whoever presents the bond, may receive the interest and principal payments.

3.7.6 Priority

Some bonds supersede others in terms of the right to be paid off. This means that in case of liquidation, some bondholders are given the privilege to be paid off first as compared to other bonds.

For e.g. the above-mentioned Second Mortgage Bonds have inferior rights over other senior bonds.

3.7.7 Repayment Provisions

a. **Income Bonds** pay interest contingent on the issuer's profitability
b. **Revenue Bonds** are paid from specific revenue sources. The terms are settled beforehand. The government normally issues these bonds.

3.8 How the Bonds risks are analyzed?

As with all risk and return theory, it is quite clear that the return from the bonds is dependent on the risk that they bear. Therefore, the more risk they carry, more the return will be demanded by the investors. We have also discussed that different types of bonds are perceived differently in terms of risk.

The question arises that how do we evaluate the risk associated with the same types of bonds offered by different issuers?

A long answer to this question is that it depends on lots of factors, which primarily includes assessing the issuer's ability to pay its debt. This can be done by analyzing factors like the issuer's financial and credit history, profitability, leverage (ratio of debt and equity), the industry trends in which he/she is operating and tons of other indicators.

The task becomes even more tiresome when you are comparing the creditworthiness of two issuers from different industries.

However, the good news is that these tedious activities are taken care of by different credit rating agencies that, from time to time, publish their ratings on different investment and non-investment rating bonds.

The most dominating of these agencies are Moody's, Standard & Poor's and Fitch and the highest ratings assigned are triple A or Aaa and the lowest is CC.

Note: The ratings published are only for the securities issued by companies and not individual debtors

Chapter 4: Capital Structure of a Business

Do you remember (it was mentioned earlier) that the profit invested back into the business is also treated as a form of equity finance and the cost of it is the same as the ordinary equity financing? In this chapter of the book we will deal with the combination of equity and debt financing within a business and how the businesses decide what ratio of both mode of financing is to be pursued when managing their finance.

4.1 Cost of Capital

Even though the Equity and Debt financing are totally different, the costs of both depend on each other.

Investors pay money to the corporation with the hope of achieving greater returns in the future (dividends). When these expectations are not met, they sell their stocks causing the stock price to fall (due to an increase in supply of the shares when compared with the demand).

Generally, declining shares price gives an impression of deteriorating business performance and the potential investors (lenders) perceive you as a risky bet. This may not be true in every case but this is how the business world works. People go for impression and when they don't receive healthy vibes, they raise their demands (in terms of rates of return) when lending their money. Hence the cost of debt is raised when you go out asking for funds.

The same goes other way around as well. When you default on your debt, the shareholders automatically presume that, standing last in queue for compensation, they will not be receiving dividends on their shares. Hence, they start selling their shares and that causes the share price to decline. Next time when you decide to raise equity finance through selling additional shares, you will not receive favorable response and therefore, you will raise less money relatively with the same amount of efforts you did previously.

In order to evaluate the cost of capital of the business, it is necessary to find out what makes up its cost or to put it more simply, what exactly are the components of cost of capital.

4.2 Components of Cost of Capital

The firm's financing structure is built upon 3 components:

a. Long term debt (Debt Financing)
b. Common Stock Equity / Ordinary Shares Equity (Equity Financing)
c. Preferred Stock Equity (Equity Financing)

Point to note:
There is one more component known as Short Term Debt that is not usually dealt with Cost of Capital. **Working Capital Management** requirements are normally met with short-term funds and are usually not considered when evaluating the firm's cost of capital. We will discuss this later in this book.

The rate of return demanded by the holder of each component

becomes the cost of that component. Therefore, in order to evaluate the firm's overall cost of capital, it is necessary to calculate the cost of each component separately.

4.2.1 Cost of Long Term Debt (LTD)

Since the interest payable on debt is tax deductible, the cost of long term debt is the after tax interest rate demanded by the providers of the debt. It can be calculated as:

Cost of LTD = Effective Rate x (1.0 – Marginal Tax Rate)

Where:

- *Effective Rate is an interest rate that also accounts for the compounding occurring more than once a year. For the sake of simplicity, just keep it to the normal interest rates in the market.*
- *Marginal Tax Rate is the tax rate paid on the additional dollar of your wealth. Again, for the sake of simplicity, let's just assume it is the normal tax rate.*

4.2.2 Cost of Preferred and Common Stock (Cost of Equity - COE)

The component cost of Equity Finance (both common and preferred) is calculated as:

COE (Common Stock) = Cash Dividend of Common Stock ÷ Market Price of Common Stock

COE (Preferred Stock) = Cash Dividend of Preferred Stock ÷ Market Price of Preferred Stock

Points to Note:
- The cost of Retained Earnings (Profits Re-Invested) is the same as the Cost of Equity (COE)
- Market Price of **total** Common Stock **upon issuance** of each class of equity is the net proceeds from the issuance (gross proceeds – floatation cost)

Example:

A firm has outstanding bonds with the stated rate of 8% and an effective rate of 6%. With the par value of USD 50.00, the 5% preferred shares are currently trading at USD 70.00 per share and its common stocks with the par value of USD 1 are being traded at USD 1.5. The dividend normally paid on the common stocks by the firm is 10% of the par value.

The applicable tax rate is 35%

What is the firm's cost of capital of each component?

Long Term Debt

Cost = Effective Rate x (1.0 – Tax Rate)

= 6% x (1.0 – 35%)

= 6% x .65

= 3.9%

Preferred Stock

Cost = Cash Dividend ÷ Market Price

= (50 x 5%) ÷ 70

= 2.5 ÷ 70

$= 3.57\%$

Common Stock

$Cost = Cash\ Dividend \div Market\ Price$

$= (1 \times 10\%) \div 1.5$

$= 0.1 \div 1.5$

$= 6.67\%$

4.3 Weighted Average Cost of Capital (WACC)

The earlier mentioned costs of capital are the costs of each component of the capital that the firm has used in order to mold its corporate capital structure.

However, it would be convenient if the company comes up with a single figure depicting its overall cost of capital.

The most convenient and intuitive way is to take the cost of each component, assign a weight to it and sum the product of its costs and their respective weight. The result will be the firm's overall cost of capital, which is also known as the Weighted Average Cost of Capital or WACC.
The weight assigned to each component is the firm's target capital structure, which is normally designated by the corporate management. For e.g. the firm might want to build its capital on the basis of 20% debt, 10% preferred capital and 70% ordinary capital.

Example

Continuing the cost of capital example above, the firm decides to set a target capital structure of 40% debt, 50% common equity and 10% preferred equity. The Weighted Average Cost of Capital (WACC) of the firm can be calculated as:

	Target Weight		Cost of Capital	Weighted Cost
Long Term Debt	50%	X	3.9%	1.95%
Preferred Equity	10%	X	3.57%	0.36%
Common Equity	40%	X	6.67%	2.67%
			WACC	4.98%

4.4 Optimal Capital Structure

When you have to source funds, the objective of each business is to minimize the cost of obtaining each pool of funds.

Life would have been easy if all that entrepreneurs had to care about was going for the option with the least amount of return required by the providers of those funds.
However, this is not the case.

As we have studied earlier, each source of funds inherit their own pluses and minuses, for e.g. the debt allows you to deduct the interest paid for taxable purpose but the equity relieves you from the regular payments to the stakeholders.

So the trickiest part is deciding with what proportion the firm's objectives should be funded with each component of capital so that the overall cost of obtaining and maintaining these funds is as its minimum. We refer to this as the optimal capital structure of the firm.

As should be becoming more evident, wealth maximizes when the WACC is at its minimum and therefore effective management of organizations is not only to focus on the maximization of Earnings per share (EPS) but also to minimize the WACC as well.

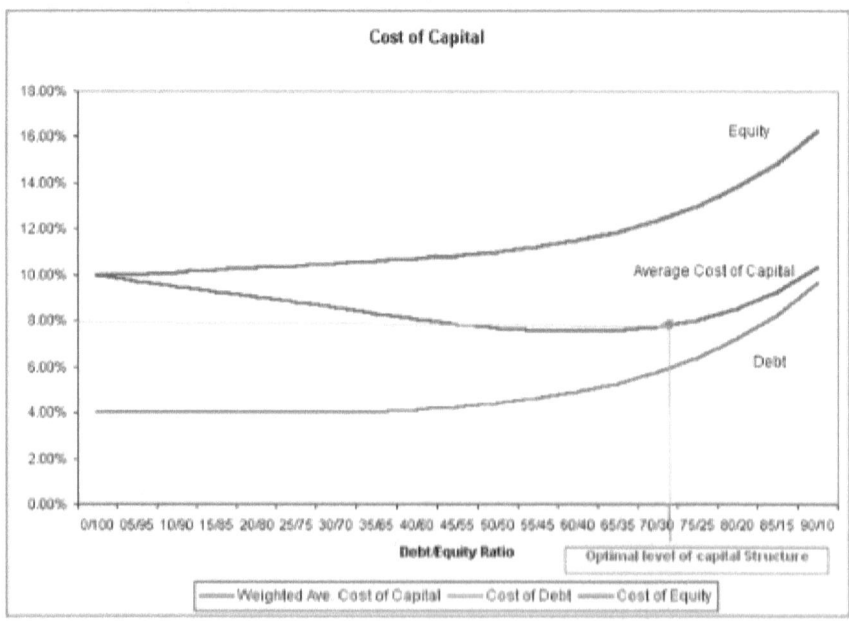

(Image Source: Accounting Education – www.svtuition.org)

It is quite difficult for firms to decide precisely what the optimal structure of their capital should be, and thus in practice they attempt to assess a range of capital structures.

4.5 Marginal Cost of Capital (MCC)

The more a firm raises capital, the more expensive it becomes for it to raise the next unit of capital. The investor demands more return because they perceive the firm to be more risky.

The marginal cost of capital is the cost of the next monetary unit of capital raised by the firm. This marginal cost rises due to the existing sources of funds being exhausted.

An example of Marginal Cost of Capital (MCC) can be understood from the following diagram where after each series of funding the cost of capital changes radically.

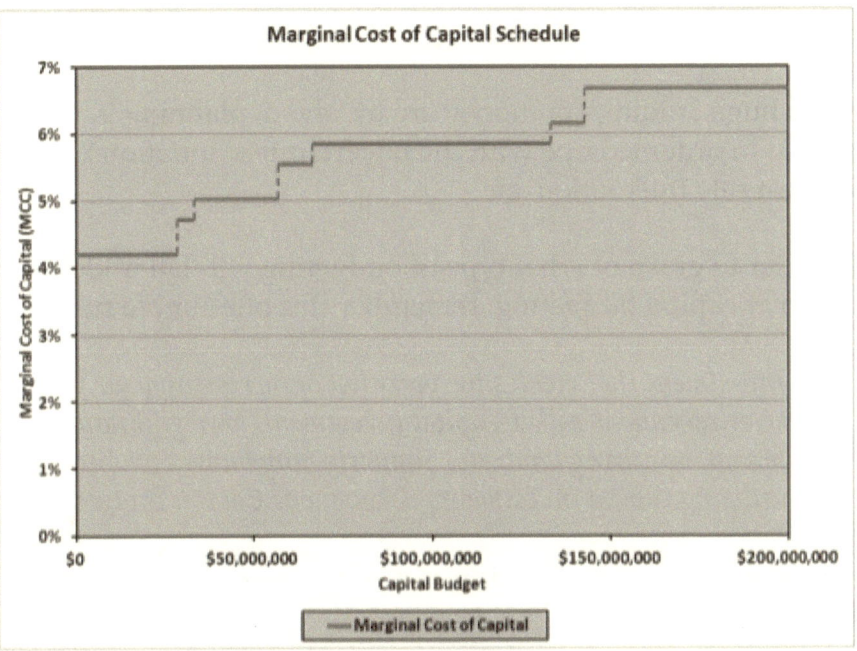

(Image Source: Financial Exam Help 123 – www.financialexamhelp123.com)

Chapter 5: Capital Budgeting

In order to raise new funds it is necessary to plan (well) in regards to: what amount of capital will be needed, what will be the capital structure and what resources will be tapped in order to fund your activities.

For this purpose, a budget is drawn so as to plan and control investments for long-term projects. This budget is called a Capital Budget and the process is known as Capital Budgeting.

A capital budget differs from normal budget as it is more long term and involves substantial sums of money in terms of expenditures.

Since huge amounts of money are involved, planning is crucial in order to cope with the uncertainties, inflation, interest rate fluctuation, etc.

In order to grasp of what type of budgeting will fall under the realm of capital budgeting, remember this one simple rule:

Any investment that creates the potential of increasing your future income or revenue is called Capital Investment, for e.g. Buying and equipment, acquiring land, etc. Similarly, any budget planned for utilizing capital investments is known as Capital Budget.

To draw a capital budget it is necessary to keep track of the Relevant Cash Flows.

5.1 Relevant Cash Flows

Relevant Cash Flows are the cash flows that arise as a result of undertaking any particular project. For any cash flow to become 'relevant' it is necessary that it occurred (and only occurred) because of that particular project, and therefore you should not include **sunk costs** that are already spent.

Identifying relevant cash flows is important to evaluate the investment. The relevant cash flows for capital budgeting are:

a. *Cost of new equipment*
b. *Annual after tax cash savings or inflows*
c. *Proceeds from disposal of old equipment.*
d. *Adjustment for depreciation expense on new equipment i.e. the tax saved as a result of the depreciation expense of the new equipment.*

Over the period of time, many methods have been developed to assess the profitability and health of a project. Some of them are:

1. *Net Present Value (NPV)*
2. *Internal Rate of Return*
3. *Payback Period*
4. *Accounting Rate of Return*
5. *Economic Value Added*

We will go through each of them one by one.

5.2 Net Present Value (NPV)

Ever heard your grandpa's complaints about how everything in his time was worth dime a dozen and how he would buy tons of supplies just from a single buck?

Well, the bitter fact is that your grandpa is not being nostalgic. Over time money loses its value and a single unit of money, now, is worth more than the same unit of money after a certain time period (in the future). This is called the devaluation of money and when it comes to financial management, we use the term **discounted**. We 'discount' the value of money from the future to assess what it is worth in today's terms.

So what does the NPV has to do with capital budgeting? NPV involves discounting the relevant cash flows using the 'required rate of return' as the discount rate.

Since capital investments involve return based on number of years, it is necessary to discount your cash flows in order to have a better picture by incorporating the effects of devaluation of money.

A capital project's net present value (NPV) is the difference between the 'present value' (discounted value) of all its cash inflows and outflows. If the discounted cash inflows are greater than the discounted outflows, *the project is accepted.*

The Present Value (PV) of 1 unit of money over "n" period of years and with a required rate of "D" can be calculated as:

$$PV = \frac{1}{(1+D)^n}$$

Example:

ABC Co. is planning to purchase equipment for US $100,000 having a useful life of 10 years with no residual value. The equipment will be installed in a plant that is already being used by the company for its other activities and ABC Co. pays a rent of US $6,000 per year on it.

The machine is expected to generate inflow of US $60,000 over its useful life and would be depreciated on a straight-line basis (annual depreciation of US $10,000).

The project's required rate of return is 12% and the effective tax rate is 35%.

Point To Note:
The Present Value (PV) of $1 for the 10th year at 12% is 0.322 and total PV from year 1 to year 10 provided that you keep receiving $1 each year (remember the ordinary annuity?) is 5.650.

Present Value of Cash Savings		US $
Annual operating cash savings/inflows		60,000
Annual Tax Expense		
Tax expense on annual cash savings 60,000 x 40%	(24,000)	
Depreciation Tax Shield 10,000 x 40%	4,000	(20,000)
After tax net annual savings		30,000
PV factor for an ordinary annuity		x 5.650
		169,500
Cost of Equipment (Required Investment)	(100,000)	

Net Present Value of Investment (NPV)	69,500

Since the NPV is positive, the project should be undertaken.
In other words, by undertaking this project you are creating $69,500 worth of value (in today's dollars!).

Note on the Depreciation Tax Shield:
Since depreciation is an allowable expense for tax purposes and a taxpayer can use it to lower their tax liability, in the above example, the investor is able to save ($10,000 x 40%) $4,000 by recognizing depreciation expenses, so a depreciation tax shield is the amount of tax you are able to save by introducing depreciation.

If you want a free capital budgeting spreadsheet that can calculate project NPVs, pro forma income statements and other information, you can access one via this link:
http://www.accofina.com/capital-budgeting-excel.html

5.3 Internal Rate of Return (IRR)

The Internal Rate of Return of a project is the discount rate at which the investment's Net Present Value is exactly 0 (zero).

Remember this, the IRR is always a percentage (a discount rate) and it gives you a benchmark in terms of the minimum return that you should be expecting (in terms of percentage) from a project, otherwise your net cash flows will be negative. As a rule of thumb, you should keep in mind that:
If the IRR of a project is greater than the 'hurdle rate' (the minimum return an investor expects from the investment), the investment is desirable and *the project should be undertaken.*

This relationship is more simplified below:

IRR > Hurdle rate = Accept project
IRR < Hurdle rate = Decline project

The IRR is calculated as:

$$IRR = r_a + \{[NPV_a \div (NPV_a - NPV_b)] \times (r_b - r_a)\%\}$$

Where:

r_a = *discount rate at which net present value (NPV) is positive*
r_b = *discount rate at which net present value (NPV) is negative*
NPV_a = *NPV at* r_a
NPV_b = *NPV at* r_b

5.4 Payback Period

The Payback Period of a project is the number of years it will take the net cash inflow to equal the original investment.

This method is used by the firms who have set a maximum length of time within which project must pay for itself in order to become acceptable.

Provided that the cash flows are constant, Payback period is calculated as:

Payback period =
Initial Investment ÷ Annual after Tax Cash Savings/inflows

Example:

ABC Co. has set a period of 3 years within which the project should recover its cost. What should be the decision of ABC Co. if an investment of $250,000 generates a cash inflow of $70,000 per year?

Payback period = $250,000 ÷ $70,000 = 3.57 years.

The project should not be accepted (as it took longer than 3 years).

If the cash flows are not constant then the calculation must be in cumulative form.

Example:

Continuing the above example but with a cash inflow of $70,000, $65,000, $90,000 and $100,000 in the years 1, 2, 3 and 4.

Period	Cash Inflows	Remaining Initial Investment
Initial Investment – Year 0	US $ -	(250,000)
Year 1	70,000	(180,000)
Year 2	65,000	(115,000)
Year 3	90,000	(25,000)
Year 4	100,000	75,000

The project payback period is 3 years and (($25000 ÷ $100,000) x 12 *months*) 3 months.

5.4.1 Upsides of Payback Period

The foremost merit of payback period is its simplicity.
In addition to its simplicity, the payback period tends to
measure the risk as well. Since the longer the period the more
risky the investment is, businesses generally keep track of the
payback periods of their investments in order to keep their
risk level under control.

5.4.2 Downsides of Payback Period

The payback period disregards the time value of money (the
devaluation, the discounting). By assigning equal weight to
each and every cash flow this ignores the fact that investments
have a time cost.

Secondly, the payback method also tends to disregard all the
cash inflows *after* the payback cutoff date. Since the only
concern of this method is to calculate the payback period, it
may create tendency of the investors towards accepting many
marginal projects and ignoring projects with healthy cash
inflows further into the future.

5.5 Accounting Rate of Return

The Accounting Rate of Return (ARR) also known as Average
Rate of Return is yet another investment appraisal method
which tends to ignore the time value of money.

This method takes into account the return generated from the
capital investment in form of a percentage return.

ARR is normally calculated as:

$ARR = (Annual\ Cash\ Inflow - Depreciation) \div Initial\ Investment$

Example:

A small retail store is planning to purchase a vending machine costing US $10,000 that would probably generate US 2,500 per year in return (after tax). The vending machine has no salvage value and the retailer believes that the useful life of the machine is around 10 years.

The ARR of the proposed vending machine is:

Return generated from the machine	$2,500.00
Depreciation per year ($10,000 ÷ 10 years)	($1,000.00)
Annual Increase in Income	$1,500.00
Initial Investment	÷ (10,000)
Accounting Rate of Return (ARR)	15.00%

5.5.1 Upsides of ARR

The advantage of using this method is that all the necessary information in order to arrive at ARR is easily available from the books maintained by the business owners.

5.5.2 Downsides of ARR

Ironically, the disadvantage of using ARR is linked with its advantage. Though the data to calculate ARR is readily available it depends a lot on the subjective values, such as choice of depreciation methods.

For e.g. the yearly depreciation expense depends a lot on the accounting method used by the business and may not represent the actual cash flows.

5.6 Economic Value Added

Economic Value Added (EVA) calculates the residual income of an investment that is in excess of the required return demanded by the business's creditors
.

Although the above statement may be self-explanatory, an example here would certainly be helpful. But before jumping to an example keep this in mind that the "Return demanded by the business's creditors" is normally considered as the Weighted Average Cost of Capital that we have already discussed above.

The reason for this is because if the firm has raised many forms of finances, WACC will be the closest assessment of the cost of capital that the firm has to pay.

Example:

Let's continue the above example of vending machine. The retailer, after expected results produced by the first vending machine decides to purchase and install another one. Again, the cost of that machine will be US $10,000.

Assuming that the business has no other form of finance to purchase the machine, decides to borrow the money from the bank with the commitment of paying US $1,500 in yearly installments. The net income generated from the vending machine is US $2,500 per year.

The retailer's EVA is:

Net Income from the vending machine	*$2,500.00*
WACC (assuming no other form of finance)	*($1,500.00)*
Economic Value Added (EVA)	*$1,000.00*

The major advantage of using this method is that EVA determines whether an investment is increasing the shareholders' value by taking into account the marginal benefits obtained by using the resources in a particular way. Therefore, EVA calculates the entity's true "Economic" benefit.

Chapter 6: Cash Management & Working Capital

All businesses (and particularly SMEs) rely heavily on cash. When we say cash, this does not mean "money" or "funds" in a rhetoric sense but actual hard cash or short-term investments that can easily be converted into cash (liquidated) on a very short-term notice.

This short-term investment is generally referred to as working capital, and management of this working capital is known as Working Capital Management.

In order to run the day-to day business, it is necessary to maintain a decent amount of cash so that short-term liabilities and expenses can be paid off and the ball keeps rolling.

However, at the same time it is also not wise at all to stock huge piles of cash to meet your working capital needs. Since idle cash does not earn return, only the amount needed to meet short-term obligations should be placed at your immediate disposal.

6.1 Why should the firm maintain a minimum balance of idle funds?

Since the idle funds do not earn return, maintaining an excessive balance of funds that are not going to be needed for immediate use is not a wise strategy.

Idle funds normally have an **"Opportunity Cost"**, i.e. the benefit forgone of investing the funds into another investment opportunity. Therefore, if you believe that maintaining unnecessary funds in your account (or petty cash) will provide you ease in meeting your day-to-day obligations, you may be wrong. You may be losing money instead (from employing it in that other investment opportunity).

Hence, the objective of Cash Management is not to maximize cash on hand but to use it in the most efficient way, and the optimal level of cash should be determined by a cost benefit analysis.

In this chapter we will look at the most common techniques that businesses follow in order to manage their cash. Additionally, some ready sources of acquiring working capital will also be our topic of interest for this chapter.

6.2 Compensating Balance

The Compensating Balance is the minimum balance that is required by the bank, from the customer, to keep in their checking account. The purpose of this balance is to compensate the bank for various services rendered to the account holder such as writing unlimited checks.

Appreciation of compensation balances is necessary as the funds submitted as a compensation balance are unavailable for the firm's use and thus incur opportunity cost.

Moreover, being short-term, it does not earn any interest as well.

For effective working capital management it is necessary that the firm have the necessary funds available whenever required. Obviously, it wouldn't be wise to apply for bank loan to pay your utility bill, therefore the major source of short-term finance is the firm's own revenue or profits. The problem is that many businesses work on a credit basis. They either pay their suppliers on a delayed basis and/or receive payments from its customers/debtors at any time later than the goods are delivered or services are rendered, and the payments behind these two activities may not coincide.

So to make sure that the firm never runs out of the minimum cash balance required it has two options. These options are either (1) to speed up cash collections from its debtors or (2) delay payments to its creditors.

6.3 Speeding up Cash Collections & Slowing Cash Disbursements

6.3.1 The Float

Even if the debtors pay on time there's still one problem. When the debtor writes a check banks normally take a day (or few) to clear the amount. This period of time between which the payer pays the check until the funds are available for use is called the float. There are various strategies employed by firms to reduce the time between selling products and receiving the cash.

6.3.2 Offering Discounts

The most popular practice of making sure that the debtors pay in time is by offering them discounts. In this way, the debtors have incentive to clear their dues on time and thus enhance certainty and cash availability on the firm's part.

Used for marketing purposes as well, this method of offering a discount also has a cost, which is the amount forgone from the discount.

6.3.3 Factoring Receivables

Factoring receivables is essentially selling your accounts receivable to another party (the factor) against immediate cash (the advance) equivalent to the face amount of the receivables.

Firms looking for immediate cash may opt for this option as they cannot afford their funds stuck with their customers for long times such as 60 or 90 days.

The factor that buys the receivables has a dedicated recovery staff that makes sure that they are able to recover the sum from the customer and hence they can operate this function more efficiently.

Once the amount is received in full, the factor hands over the sum to the firm and charges a fee for its service, the advance provided and the interest on the amount provided in advance. The financing cost is usually high in factoring arrangements.

One added advantage of factoring receivables is that the (selling) firm can cut down its expense on a credit department and accounts receivable staff.

Normally, there are two practices in factoring receivables that are followed in businesses.

1. **Recourse Factoring:** In this arrangement, the entity is responsible for the unpaid invoices (bad debts) i.e. the firm will have to buy back the invoices which are not paid by its customers.

Normally, the class of receivables with the least amount of risk to default is factored out on recourse factoring arrangement.

2. **Non-Recourse Factoring:** This is exactly opposite of recourse factoring which provides no option for the factor to claim back the unpaid invoices from the firm. Consequently, the finance charges are the highest in this mode of financial arrangement.

6.3.4 Lock Box System

A facility provided by banks, the Lock Box System, involves customers submitting their payments to a post office box rather than a bank.

The Lock Box System has strong utility for the businesses that are running businesses nationwide. Against a flat monthly fee, a bank provides a lock box arrangement based on the firm's customer population pattern.

6.3.5 Draft

When you need to slow down your cash disbursements, one way of doing is to pay through draft.

A draft is a third party instrument in which the drawer (the business) orders a drawee to pay funds to the third person (for e.g. the supplier).

One form of draft is also a check in which the drawee is a bank.

The payer uses this form of payment to delay payments.

Drafts can be drawn in advance of the due date of the invoice that will only be processed by the drawee (the bank) at the due date, thereby eliminating the necessity of writing a check earlier than the due date. This delays the outflow of the cash for the payer.

6.3.6 Payable through Draft (PTD)

Though the name sounds similar the nature of this instrument is slightly different than an ordinary draft that we discussed above.

Unlike the draft, the drawee in a PTD is the payer (the business) and they are liable to deposit sufficient funds to cover PTD when the payee (the supplier) submits the PTD to the bank.

PTD allows the firms to maintain only the minimum balance required by the bank. The funds are transferred when demanded by the payee.

On the other hand, the drawback of this instrument is that the payee usually wants to receive an instrument that will be paid on demand without any possible delay.

The second downside is that bank charges are higher for PTD services.

6.3.7 Zero Balance Account (ZBA)

Another facility provided by banks, the ZBA means that at the end of the day the bank transfers just enough funds from the firm's main account to cover all the checks presented at the Zero Balance Account all throughout that day. Thus this type of checking account (the ZBA) will continually have a zero balance (lowering excess balance opportunity costs) as it only has funds to cover that day's disbursements.

The advantage of maintaining a ZBA is that the firm can now place a higher amount of idle funds in its main account in order to avail any short-term investment opportunity and have a better overview, with improved cash control, of all its available cash (within the main account) by removing multiple balances (with possible excessive balances) in multiple accounts all over the place. The technique of utilizing a 'main' account is a form of 'cash concentration'.

6.3.8 Disbursement Float

In order to stretch the disbursement float period, sometimes the payer mails the check to the vendor while being unsure if sufficient funds would be available in order to cover the check.

For these situations, some banks offer overdraft protection services in which the bank guarantees to cover any shortfall in the disbursement funds up to a certain level.

Since the bank charges a fee against this service, one should only use it after carefully analyzing the costs between the overdraft charges and the service charges of the bank.

6.4 Spontaneous Financing

Spontaneous financing is the amount of current liabilities and accrued expenses that arise during the normal course of business without the firm's personnel needing to take deliberate actions, for e.g. salaries, taxes payable, interest, dividends, trade credits, etc.

A firm may take steps to extend the payments of these and thus are able to generate an interest free loan for themselves for the time period till the payments are delayed.

One form of spontaneous financing that can be manipulated in one owns benefit is the *trade discount*.

6.5 To Take or Not To Take a Discount?

Everyone likes discounts. They can easily entice you and when the question arises of whether to avail the discount offered by the trade creditors, an impulsive answer would be "hell yeah!"

However, this may not be the only consideration, it is possible that the short term funds that you have raised for next few days by foregoing a discount can be used in an a short term investment that yields a return more than the benefit that the trade credit discount had to offer.

In order to evaluate that which option is more beneficial, you need to know the cost of not taking discount.

$$\text{Cost of not taking discount} = \frac{\text{Discount \%}}{1 - \text{Discount \%}} \times \frac{\text{Days in year}}{\text{Total Payment Period} - \text{Discount Period}}$$

Example:

A Vendor offers merchandise to you on terms of 1/10, net 30, this means that 1% discount is available on payments within 10 days or the entire balance is due within 30 days.

You decide to forgo the discount in order to raise a spontaneous finance for the next 20 days by paying on the 30th day. Assuming 360 days in a year.

The cost that you had to bear by not taking discount is:

Cost of not taking discount

$= [1\% \div (100\% - 1\%)] \times [360 \text{ days} \div (30 \text{ days} - 10 \text{ days})]$

$= (1\% \div 99\%) \times (360 \text{ days} \div 20 \text{ days})$

$= 1.01\% \times 18$

$= 18.18\%$

You will have to bear a cost of 18.18% if you do not take a discount.

However, on the other hand, if you can invest in any short-term opportunity yielding more than 18.18% you will not lose anything by letting go the discount.

6.6 Short Term Financing Arrangements.

Quite often businesses fall short when it comes to having enough investment funds available for all the opportunities on offer. No matter how efficiently the funds are being managed, sooner or later almost all firms have to go out in search for extra funding because profits alone are not sufficient to finance some of the business objectives. Say for e.g. a planned expansion.

In that case, the most readily available providers of funds turn out to be the commercial banks.

Often you have to approach banks in search of finance that is required only for a relatively short amount of time.

Commercial banks can offer a short-term facility in the form of:

1. **Term Loan** *must be paid by a definite time.*
2. **Line of Credit** *a continuous source of borrowing for the firm up to a certain limit often referred to as a ceiling.*

As there is no free lunch, the bank charges the borrowers against this "help" in the form of interest on the principal amount.

This interest is based on the pre-determined rate on the principal amount and is also called the "stated rate".

However, often you will hear the term, "effective interest rate" on the amount of loan borrowed. Being the same as the normal interest rate in many cases, the effective interest rate can be slightly different than the normal interest rate.

6.7 Effective Interest Rate

Effective Interest Rate or Effective Rate is the ratio of the amount the firm must pay to the amount it gets use of.

Effective Interest Rate
= Interest Paid ÷ Net Proceeds or Usable Funds

If you find the above definition slightly complicated then don't worry, here's what it actually means:

Example:

A firm, looking for short-term finance, goes to the bank to borrow US $10,000 at an annual interest rate of 8%. The bank provides firm with the money but charges US $1,000 as loan processing and other necessary fees.

Effectively speaking, firm never got the full US $10,000 to use. However, the amount of interest to be paid remains the same 8%. Obviously, this is not rate that the firm is actually paying on its borrowing. Its effective interest rate will be:

Effective Interest Rate

= *(8% x $10,000) ÷ ($10,000 - $1,000)*

= *$800 ÷ $9,000*

= *8.89%*

Because of the reduction in the total amount of money available for use by the firm, the effective interest is higher because the interest is payable on the principal amount and not on the sum actually available for use.

Knowledge of effective interest rates is important because in it helps you to plan well and to figure out that how much funds you actually need. Additionally, it also helps you to deduce the true cost of your funds.

Talking of interest, banks normally charge two forms of interest on their lending.

i.   **Simple Interest Short Term Loan:** *is one in which the interest is paid at the end of the loan term. The amount of the interest to be paid is based on the stated rate and the principal of the loan (amount needed).*

Its calculation is quite simple:

Interest Expense = *Principal amount x stated rate*

ii. **Discounted Loan**: *is one in which the interest and finance charges are paid at the beginning at the of the loan term. Since the borrower does not receive the full amount of principal due to the deductions, effective interest rates on discounted loans are always higher than the nominal or stated rates.*

Additionally, when borrowing on a discounted loan arrangement, you must always be careful to include the interest being paid at the beginning when you calculate the how much funds is needed from the loan.

Total borrowing needed in case of discounted loans can be calculated as:

Total Borrowings = *Amount needed ÷ (1 – Stated rate)*

Example:

You need to pay an invoice of $50,000 and decide to borrow the sum from the bank that has extended you an offer with an interest of 8% on a discounted loan.

The total amount of money that you'd need to borrow from the bank in order to take care of the invoice and pay the interest at the beginning of the loan term as well will be:

Total Borrowings

= $50,000 ÷ (1 – 8%)

= $50,000 \div 0.92$

= $ 54,348 (rounded to the nearest unit)

Similarly, the effective interest rate on your above borrowings will be:

Effective Rate

= ($54,348 x 8%) \div $50,000

= $4,348 \div $50,000

= 8.7%

6.8 Loans with a Compensating Balance

As mentioned earlier, a compensating balance is the minimum amount of money required by the banks to be deposited in the bank in order to meet daily funds requirements or to reduce the risk (for the bank and you) that you run out of available funds.

When borrowing, banks may require certain amount of money to be placed in the account as compensating balance. Again, consideration must be given to the compensating balance as well, because the amount available for use will be lower than initially foreseen and hence you will still be short of cash despite the borrowing.

Similarly, because the borrower gets to use a lower amount than what is actually borrowed on the paper, effective interest rates on loans with compensating balances are higher than the stated interest rates.

The calculations to ascertain the exact amount of principal and the effective interest rate are:

Total Borrowings
= Amount needed ÷ (1 – Compensating balance %)

Example:

A supplier has offered you a discount of 1% if the invoice of $25,000 is paid in within the next 10 days. You want to avail the discount but don't have enough money hence decided to go to the bank for the borrowing.

The bank has offered a loan with a stated rate of 10% but has also embedded a requirement of compensating balance of 8% of the principal amount.

The actual amount of borrowing that you need to make is:

Total borrowing

= Amount needed ÷ (1.0 – Compensating balance %)

= ($25,000 x 99%) ÷ (1.0 – 8%)

= $24,750 ÷ 0.92

= $26,902

Since you get to use lower amount of money than what you will actually borrow so the effective interest rate is higher than the stated interest rate:

Effective Rate *= Interest Expense ÷ Funds available for use*

= ($26,902 x 10%) ÷ $25,000

= $2,690.2 ÷ $25,000

= 10.8%

To ease up your life, you don't always need to go through the trouble of calculating the "amount needed" figure first to calculate the effective rate as this can be done even without going through this trouble.

All you need is the stated rate and the rate of compensating balance:

Effective Rate

= *Stated Rate ÷ (1.0 – Compensating balance %)*

= *10% ÷ (1.0 – 8%)*

= *10% ÷ (0.92)*

= *10.8%*

6.9 Secured Financing:

In secured financing, the lender (normally a bank) offers credit to the borrower and secures it by backing it up through the borrower's assets.

a. *One way of doing so is by* **pledging receivables.**
   In this form of secured financing arrangement, the firm commits to use the proceeds from its receivables to pay off its loan.

The bank normally lends up to 80% of the outstanding receivables and may seek more of a guarantee that the receivables won't default by assessing the average age of the accounts and the likelihood of their collectability.

b. *In* **Warehouse Financing** *a firm's inventory is used as a security of the loan. This is done in either of the two ways.*

i. A third party, say a public warehouse holds the inventory and serves as the agent of the creditor. The creditor receives a receipt of the warehouse as evidence of stake of the borrower in the asset.

ii. A field warehouse is established when the warehouse take the possession of the inventory on the debtor's property. The inventory is released as needed for sale.

6.10 Chapter Conclusion

Once you realize that you have enough money to play with it's always wise to make sure that not all your eggs are in one basket.

This may sound simple but it requires careful evaluation of different types of investments that we've already discussed earlier.

When investments are made, they may yield you profits or you may end up in incurring a loss. That's all part of the game. But a wise guy always keeps exploring opportunities with minimum risks and maximum return.

Risk management attempts to keep the level of risk within your risk appetite. Every effective financial management requires a well-studied risk management plan in order to make sure that your investments are handled in the safest way possible.

We know that the term 'risk management plan' may be too boring and dry. In fact, these could be the reasons why you skipped your accounting and finance classes in the first place.

So don't worry, we won't go deep in this labyrinth but it is also necessary to get you acquaint with the nuts and bolts of risk management. It will be very short and concise. We promise that.

Chapter 7: Managing Your Risks

The objective of risk management is not to eliminate risk, as it can never be completely eliminated. Of course, how would you generate a return if there were no risk? After all, if there was no risk, then everyone would do it and everyone would make a return …and effectively we would have finally found that elusive 'money tree'!

As the name suggests, the main purpose of risk management is to make attempts to diffuse the adverse effects of a negative outcome so that if anything goes wrong, you are in a position to deal with it (without going broke).

This is a very simple definition of risk management and, as a matter of fact, big corporations invest major portions of their corporate income in maintaining departments whose sole purpose is to keep a check on the level of risk and make sure that it does not go beyond their risk appetites.

7.1 Basics of Risk Management

There a four standard methods of managing risk:

7.1.1 Risk Acceptance

This is the most basic risk management step that any entrepreneur does. In fact, it is simply nothing but a businessman undergoing and accepting risk.

In investment terms, it means that the costs of managing a certain type of activity is simply accepted, for e.g. not changing your plans and making an investment or undertaking a project.

7.1.2 Risk Avoidance

Totally the opposite of accepting risk, this risk management method is taken when a risk associated with any activity is too much to bear and you consider that the cost of any risk outweighs the benefits of the opportunity.

If this is the case, then simply avoid the said activity. For e.g. rejecting a proposal or choosing not to do a business in a particular location.

7.1.3 Risk Reduction

This strategy aims to lower the level of risk associated with an activity. In this method a risky activity is undergone but attempts are made to lower the likelihood of that risk.

The best example of this would be installing a robust anti-virus and overall information security systems for your system in order to avoid penetration and leakage of your business data.

7.1.4 Risk Sharing

This strategy transfers some of the loss to another party. There are different ways in which a business can share risks with others.

The most prominent of them are insurance, hedging, etc. Another example is when you partner with someone as a joint venture ...you are actually sharing risks with partners.

7.2 Derivatives

Just like other financial instruments such as cash, accounts receivables, bonds, etc. derivatives are also financial instruments.

A derivative instrument is an investment transaction in which the gain or loss of the parties is derived from another economic event, for example a change in the price of any product, currency exchange rates, etc.

When two parties bind themselves in a contract involving a derivative instrument, it usually depicts the fact that one party enters in to the transaction for speculation purpose and other for hedging purpose.

7.3 Hedging

The processing of gaining cover against potential risks is called hedging.

Usually offsetting commitments are used in order to gain this objective. This means that a person takes position in a financial instrument, which is almost perfectly correlated with the price of some other asset, but in the opposite direction.

With respect to other entity's assets, a person can acquire any one of the following positions:

1. *Long Position: When a person owns the asset he is said to be in the long position. If the market value of the acquired asset goes up, the person benefits directly from it.*

2. *Short Position: When a person sells an asset that he does not own, then he is said to acquire short position in that asset.*

Although, the "Short Position" gig sounds a bit counter-intuitive but here's what the deal is. The person sells an asset without owning them. This can be done with different financial instruments like shares, etc. But the seller normally borrows them from their real owners. Once sold, the seller expects the market value of the asset to go down so that he can buy and return those assets back to its real owners. This is commonly known as "Short Selling" and a short seller expects that the value of the asset will go down in the near future.

Example:

Mr. A is a shrewd businessman and he believes that the company XYZ's shares are going to plummet possibly because of losses that the company will incur. Mr. A decides to sell shares of XYZ Company in the stock exchange. However, he does not plan to buy them any time sooner.

In fact, looking at the future decrease in prices, Mr. A decides to short sell the shares.

- *If the price of XYZ Company decreases, Mr. A will buy back the shares and return them back to its owner. His profit will be the difference between the selling price and the purchase price.*
- *However, if Mr. A makes a mistake, and the share price instead of going down, it goes up, then Mr. A will incur a loss.*

If you wish to learn more about analyzing businesses (to help predict if stocks will rise or fall) then you may be interested in another accofina book, "Ratio Analysis Fundamentals: How 17 Financial Ratios Can Allow You to Analyse Any Business on the Planet". You can find this book at Amazon via this link: **http://www.amazon.com/gp/product/B00AIJU1X4/**

Since everything explained in the above example is based on a businessperson's hunch, there is always great amount of uncertainty lurking around. So it is necessary to hedge your bet. You can do this by investing in another asset that is perfectly correlated, but in opposite direction, so that any loss incurred is offset.

Some of the financial instruments that are used for hedging are:

7.3.1 Options

An Option is actually a right to demand that the seller/writer of the option buy or sell the underlying asset on or before a specified date (the expiration date).

So the buyer pays the fee to gain the right of dictating terms in the future whether the seller buys or sells the underlying asset from or to the buyer.

The buyer of the option is called the holder of the option and the seller is normally called the writer.

There are two major types of options:

1. *Call Option: This gives the buyer the right to purchase (or as the name suggests, "call") the underlying asset at a fixed price.*

2. **Put Option:** *This gives the holder the right to sell the underlying asset at a fixed price to the writer.*

The writer does not have a choice in an option. He has to do what the holder requires on or before the specified date. However, an option only remains valid till the expiration date. Beyond this date, the option cannot be exercised.

7.3.1.1 Components of an Option's Price

An option's price is made up of two components:

- *Intrinsic Value*
- *Time Premium (also called the Extrinsic Value).*

Before explaining these two components, it is necessary to review once again what the exercise price of an option is, as it keeps on slightly changing based on the nature of the option.

An exercise price of a:

- **Call Option:** *The **price** at which the holder of an option can **buy the underlying asset from the writer.***

- **Put Option:** *The **price** at which the holder of an option can **sell the underlying asset to the writer.***

The intrinsic value of an option is dependent on the exercise price of the option so much so that in fact it is actually derived from it, and again, it also slightly changes its definition based on the nature of the option (call or put).

For a Call Option, its intrinsic value is the amount by which the **exercise price is less than the current price of the underlying asset**. If the intrinsic value is in **positive**, the option is said to be **in-the-money**. Otherwise, it is called **out-of-the-money**.

Example:

You hold a call option of 100 shares in ABC Co. having exercise price of US $98 per share. ABC's shares are currently trading at US $100 per share. The option you hold have an intrinsic value of:

> **Intrinsic Value of a Call Option**
>
> *= Current price – Exercise price*
>
> *= $100 - $98*
>
> *= $2 per share*

The option is in-the-money. Had the shares been trading at a price more than its exercise price of option of US $100, the option would have been out-of-the-money as you would have no benefit exercising your right on the option. Hence the intrinsic value of the option would have been $0.

For a put option, its intrinsic value is the amount by which the exercise price is greater than the current price of the underlying asset. If the intrinsic value is in **positive**, the option is said to be **in-the-money**. Otherwise, it is **out-of-the-money**.

Example:

Carrying forward the above example, now you hold put options of

100 shares of ABC Co. trading at US $98 per share. You have the exercise price of $100 per share on the put options. In this case, the intrinsic value of a put option is:

> **Intrinsic Value of a Put option**
>
> = *Exercise Price − Current Price*
>
> = *$100 - $98*
>
> =$2

Again, the (put) option is in-the-money but this time the exercise price is greater than the current price. In the other case (the current price being higher than the exercise price), you would have no current benefit holding the put option as by exercising your right on it (i.e. by demanding the writer to buy it on lower price than the market rate), you would've incurred loss and hence the intrinsic value would have been US $0.

7.3.2 Forward Contract

Another financial instrument to hedge the risk on your investment, a forward contract, involves two parties agreeing that on a specified future date, one of them will perform an action and the other party will pay a specified amount for that action.

Sounding similar to options, forward contracts are slightly different as in options, the holder of the option has the *right* to whether exercise his privilege or not. But in forward contract, both parties *have to* meet their contractual obligation.

Example:

While finalizing your business deal with an international supplier, you settle on terms that a payment of UK £10,000 will be paid 1 month from now for the raw material supplied today. The current currency exchange rate of UK to US is £1.00 = $1.20.

The currency rate after 1 month is expected to be £1.00 = $1.25. Realizing that UK pound will become expensive in one-month time, you entered in a forward contract today with a currency dealer.

Terms have been decided that the currency dealer will provide UK pounds for the rate of $1.22 i.e. £1.00 = $1.22 during the time of payment.

At the date of the payment, if the exchange rate turns out to be the expected £1.00 = $1.25 then you would make a profit of:

£10,000 x ($1.25 – $1.22)

= $300

In this way, you have managed to secure your short term financing by entering in the forward contract.

However, did you notice one thing in the above example? The forward contract was entered on the basis of an expectation that something would happen in the future. Our example dealt with the case when the things happened as you expected and you saved $300 or in other words, you managed to **"hedge"** your $300.

But what if the exchange rate had turned out to move totally in the opposite direction?

Of course, you would have incurred loss on it, but that would have been the 'cost' involved in receiving the earlier certainty created by your forward contract (the hedge locked in a set outcome from an earlier point in time).

7.3.3 Futures Contract

The basics of futures contract are similar to those of forward contracts however, unlike forward contracts, the counterparty is unknown.

The reason being is that these contracts are actively traded on the futures exchanges. With the help of an intermediary, known as a Clearing House, the exchange traded futures use this clearinghouse to constantly keep looking for sellers who will deliver in the given period and helps them meet with the buyers who are seeking delivery during the same period.

Since the futures are actively traded in the exchanges, they are considered to be highly liquid.

7.4 Chapter Conclusion

Above are some of the hedging instruments that may help you in covering your investments and managing risk, but remember, mere knowledge of these instruments is not sufficient to protect you from the mishaps.

As business is a skill that one acquires over time through his experience with failures and successes, these hedging instruments are as safe as your business knowledge.

Just like the driver and the car analogy where even the safest car is as safe as its driver is cautious, these instruments are also beneficial to the extent that you know how and when to use them. Therefore, we suggest you to keep honing your skills as much as possible.

Summary

We have tried to give you, although brief, a comprehensive overview of how the financial management aspect of business is normally taken care of. With the hope that this book kindles your desire to dive deeper in this domain, we encourage you to read further books written by reputed writers in order to enhance your knowledgebase.

Before concluding and winding up, let us summarize the topics that we have discussed throughout this book.

As this book is meant to be an 'easy read' and since it is lot easier to grasp a concept when you are following it in a logical sequence, let's go through all the topics above very swiftly.

Below, we are jotting down the whole summary of the book but not in a dull robotic way. Let's assume that you are going out to raise finance for your business.

Now, you are in the right mindset to follow the below steps so go on and read the summary below but remember one thing! Business favors flexibility and that is what we want you to be in your approach. The below points mentioned are just to guide you. It's not necessary that you will always have to follow these points in the same manner. Certainly, you can skip any step and shuffle up their order as long as they suit your business needs.

Additionally, the below perspective we have followed is of the person who needs to raise finance for their business but it can be other way around as well. You may be saving the day for other businesspeople by investing in their businesses. Even in this case the summary below is going to be helpful for you.

1. You decide to start a new business. The best approach to choose your domain is the **risk and benefit approach**. Make sure that you go for the niche with maximum return with the least amount of risk.

2. One way of evaluating your return is by using the **"Return on Income (ROI)"** criteria. If it's a single investment opportunity, use **"ROI in absolute terms"** and if you have more than one project for evaluation, then go for **"ROI in percentage terms"**. However, calculating both won't hurt you a bit.

3. Moreover, an acquaintance of "**types of risk**" that can affect your return is also necessary. Don't let this knowledge go in vain. Apply it and carefully analyze each and every risk associated with all the investments or business plans on your desk.

4. Now you've made your decision and you plan to raise additional finance for your new business, you have to decide between **"Debt Finance"** and **"Equity Finance"**.

5. **One way to raise "Debt finance"** is through issuing **"bonds"**. However, you can also invest and buy bonds being issued by other entities.

6. Whenever there are bonds lurking around, you will almost always find interest associated in tandem with them. Either you receive interests on bonds you bought

or you have to pay them on the bonds you have issued. But this interest isn't paid all at once. You have to "amortize" them over the bond's life.

7. Check what sort of bond will be best according to your business needs as there are **different bonds based on their different features.**

8. Also make sure that you **"analyze risks on bonds".**

9. Over the bond's term you have to pay the collection of principal and interest amounts at pre-determined regular intervals. These payments are called **"annuities".** Either you pay **"ordinary annuities"** or **"annuity dues"** over the life of the bonds.

10. The amount of interest payments on the bonds is affected by the decision of the issuer and if he or she is **"issuing the bonds at premium or at discount".**

11. Again, whether **"premium"** or **"discount",** you need to **"amortize"** the whole amount over the life of the bond.

12. You've decided to explore other financial options as well. Check them out! You've got heap of other financial options, but wait…! You need to make sure that you know the **risk and return associated with each financial option.**

13. The counterpart of **"Debt Financing"** is **"Equity Financing".** You may need it when you don't mind giving up some control over your business.

14. Two common ways of raising equity finance is through "**common stocks**" and "**preferred stocks**"

15. Once you've acquired capital (finance) for your business you need to evaluate the overall combined **cost of capital** through the **Capital Asset Pricing Model.**

16. Also, you should be calculating the "**components of cost of capital**" which includes the "**cost of long term debt, preferred stock**" and "**common stock**".

17. Once done, you need to calculate the overall cost of capital also known as "**Weighted Average Cost of Capital (WACC)**"

18. Additionally, you also need to decide the **optimum capital structure** for your business as well.

19. No matter what proportion of capital structure you maintain, keep an eye on your "**Marginal Cost of Capital**" as it tends to rise with every unit of finance raised.

20. One important aspect of planning to manage your finance is "**Capital Budgeting**" which helps you in deciding about your future requirements of funds.

21. In order to plan your "**capital budget**", you need to keep an eye on your "**Relevant Cash Flows**".

22. Evaluate the profitability and length of your project

through different evaluation methods including **"Net Present Value (NPV), Internal Rate of Return (IRR), Payback Period, Accounting Rate of Return and Economic Value Added (EVA)"**.

23. In managing your day-to-day business, you need to **"manage your working capital"** effectively.

24. The basic tenet of **"Working Capital Management"** is to have minimum amount of **"idle funds"** in your hands.

25. When reaching out for additional funds to banks, make sure that you inquire about any **"compensating balances"** that may be required by them.

26. Make sure that you effectively manage your day-to-day finance (working capital) by reducing the float.

27. This can be done by **"speeding up collections"** and **"delaying payments"**.

28. There are many ways in which you can reduce float. For e.g. by **"Factoring Receivables"**, utilizing a **"Lock Box System"**, paying through **"Draft"** and using **"Payable Through Draft (PTD)"**, maintaining **Zero Balance Account (ZBA)** and a **"Disbursement Float"**.

29. However, you can also take advantage of some **"Spontaneous Financing"**

30. Discounts sound good. But make sure that you have reached to the decision of **"whether you take the**

discount or not" by carefully evaluating all the cost and benefits.

31. Down the road, you may need to exploit some additional **"Short Term Financing Arrangements"** in order to meet your funds requirements. Make sure you have access to them.

32. While doing so, you must know what **"Effective Interest Rates"** you are borrowing money on. Remember, it can be different than the interest rate you are actually supposed to pay on your borrowings officially and there's a fair chance that you may be paying more on your borrowings than what is stated on the documents.

33. Always expect that banks may demand for a **"Collateral"** when going for secured financing in order reduce risk on their lending.

34. An average American millionaire has 7 sources of income. Did you notice what they just did there? They **"Managed Their Risks"**. That's what you should be doing. Don't put all your eggs in one basket.

35. Learn how to **"Reduce, Avoid, and Transfer Risk"**. Even when you have to **"Accept Risk"**, make sure that everything is meticulously calculated.

36. A well judged decision about whether to take **"Long"** or **"Short"** Position in your investments could really

make you some good money at the end of the day.

37. However, on and off, you may need to **"Hedge Your Investments"**. Some of the common hedging methods are by purchasing **"Options"**, entering into **"Forward Contracts"** or dealing in **"Futures"**.

Extras

Book Excerpt

The book you just read was targeted at entrepreneurs, business owners and business students (among others). As businesspeople we often need to seek both counsel and inspiration from leaders in our field and those from history.

Axel Tracy, the founder of accofina, felt the same way and was driven to edit a book of his favourite entrepreneurial and business quotations. Written for any entrepreneur or prospective entrepreneur, *"331 Great Quotes for Entrepreneurs: You Dream, You Believe, You Create & You Succeed"* aims to inspire, uplift and guide by offering wisdom from leaders of today and yesterday.

Below is an excerpt from this book. If you enjoy the excerpt and want to buy the book, you can find it at Amazon via this link: **http://www.amazon.com/dp/B00F2ONFO2/**

Planning & Organisational Strategy

Editor's Note:
Being able to articulate a strategy and plan is one of the first steps you must take as an entrepreneur, and then continually monitoring and updating these will be just as important. Your idea and business is obviously based on a vision you have on what will occur in the future, and being able to achieve this

vision and reach your goals is the benefit of having good plans and strategies. These quotes will remind you how important these processes and skills are and guide you through your own developments.

"Lack of direction, not lack of time, is the problem. We all have twenty-four hour days."
Zig Ziglar *(1926 – 2012) American salesman, author & motivational speaker*

"The best time to plant a tree was 20 years ago. The second best time is now."
Chinese Proverb

"Strategy is not the consequence of planning, but the opposite: its starting point."
Henry Mintzberg *(1939 -) Canadian academic & author*

"One important key to success is self-confidence. An important key to self-confidence is preparation."
Arthur Ashe *(1943 – 1993) American tennis player*

"No wind is of service to him that is bound for nowhere."
French Proverb

"You don't need to have a 100-person company to develop that idea."
Larry Page *(1973 -) American founder of Google*

"A good plan, violently executed now, is better than a perfect plan next week."
George S. Patton *(1885 – 1945) American general*

"Everyone has a plan - until they get punched in the face."
Mike Tyson *(1966 -) American boxer*

"First comes thought; then organisation of that thought, into

ideas and plans; then transformation of those plans into reality. The beginning, as you will observe, is in your imagination."
Napoleon Hill *(1883 – 1970) American author & motivational speaker*

"Planning is bringing the future into the present so that you can do something about it now."
Alan Lakein *American author*

"The general who wins the battle makes many calculations in his temple before the battle is fought. The general who loses makes but few calculations beforehand."
Sun Tzu *(544 – 496 BCE) Chinese general*

"He, who could foresee affairs three days in advance would be rich for thousands of years."
Chinese Proverb

"We don't have a traditional strategy process, planning process like you'd find in traditional technical companies. It allows Google to innovate very, very quickly, which I think is a real strength of the company."
Eric Schmidt *(1955 -) American engineer & businessperson*

"When I have one week to solve a seemingly impossible problem, I spend six days defining the problem. Then, the solution becomes obvious."

Albert Einstein *(1879 – 1955) Swiss-American Nobel-laureate physicist*

"Do not repeat the tactics which have gained you one victory, but let your methods be regulated by the infinite variety of circumstances."
Sun Tzu *(544 – 496 BCE) Chinese general*

"Planning is bringing the future into the present so that you can do something about it now."
Alan Lakein *American author*

"As for the future, your task is not to foresee it, but to enable it."
Antoine de Saint-Exupery *(1900 – 1944) French writer and aviator*

"Before you journey, observe the wind carefully, detect its direction, and then follow it. You will get to your destination twice as fast with half the effort."
Chin-Ning Chu *(1947 – 2009) Chinese-American businessperson & author*

"Strategy without tactics is the slowest route to victory. Tactics without strategy is the noise before defeat."
Sun Tzu *(544 – 496 BCE) Chinese general*

"Reduce your plan to writing. The moment you complete this, you will have definitely given concrete form to the intangible desire."
Napoleon Hill *(1883 – 1970) American author & motivational speaker*

"Someone's sitting in the shade today because someone planted a tree a long time ago."
Warren Buffett *(1930 -) American investor & Chairman Berkshire Hathaway*

"A pint of sweat will save a gallon of blood."
George S. Patton *(1885 – 1945) American general*

Free accofina.com Resources

'accofina' is the business behind this book and within its website, accofina.com, you will find a number of free resources available for download or for use on-site:

Accounting Introduction PDF mini-book *"Accounting: Foundation Inputs & Outputs"* is a 15-page PDF mini-book which is available for download. It offers some of the basic accounting theory into the inputs and outputs of a financial accounting system. The outputs are the three main financial statements and the inputs being the theory behind accounting data entry.

Find this Free Book here:

http://accofina.com/accounting-foundations.html

Capital Budgeting Spreadsheet This book covered capital budgeting earlier. You can access a spreadsheet that does a lot of number crunching and provides NPVs, pro forma income statements as well as other information just be inputting some key project data.

Find this Free Spreadsheet here:

http://accofina.com/capital-budgeting-excel.html

Time Value of Money Spreadsheet The author also spoke about the devaluation of money and present values. This available spreadsheet calculates some of the primary time value of money concepts such as future values, present values and annuities. All formulae are also provided within.

Find this Free Spreadsheet here:

http://accofina.com/time-value-money-excel.html

Ratio Analysis Spreadsheet You will find 17 of the most common financial ratios have been put into a MS Excel Spreadsheet which both calculates the ratios as well as offering the formulae behind them.

Find this Free Spreadsheet here:

http://www.accofina.com/ratio-analysis-excel.html

Cash Flow Forecast Spreadsheet The final spreadsheet offered by accofina is a 2-year monthly cash flow forecast to assist in planning and control. It provides a strong overview of 24-months and also calculates running balances, aggregate totals and overdraft interest.

Find this Free Spreadsheet here:

http://accofina.com/cash-flow-forecast-excel.html

Online Finance Calculators accofina.com has 25 on-site finance calculators available for use for free. There is some crossover with this book along with a number of other finance, business and investment calculators. They are simple JavaScript calculators where you simply enter the financial data and the calculator displays the result. A brief guidance explanation is also offered with all calculators.

Find these Free Calculators here:

http://accofina.com

More Books and Other accofina Products

More Books:

1) Ratio Analysis Fundamentals
http://www.amazon.com/gp/product/B00AIJU1X4/

2) 331 Great Quotes for Entrepreneurs
http://www.amazon.com/dp/B00F2ONFO2

3) Balance Sheet Basics
www.amazon.com/gp/product/B00EB4CBN0/

4) Income Statement Basics
www.amazon.com/gp/product/B00KUQQYUO/

Online Courses and Tutorials:

1) Financial Statement Fundamentals (Udemy Course)
https://www.udemy.com/financial-statement-fundamentals/?couponCode=34percentoff

2) Udemy Instructor Page
www.udemy.com/u/axeltracy/

3) YouTube
www.youtube.com/accofina

iOS Apps:

1) Ratio Analysis & Management Accounting Calculators

https://itunes.apple.com/au/app/ratio-analysis-management/id590212696

2) Ratio Analysis & Management Accounting Calculators 'Lite'
https://itunes.apple.com/au/app/ratio-analysis-management/id806036439

3) Profitable Pricing
http://appstore.com/profitablepricing

accofina Contact Details and Review Request

You can contact Axel Tracy at accofina anytime and for any reason at any of these contact points. Tell me if you enjoyed the book, or if you could suggest anything for a 2nd edition.

Email: **axel@accofina.com**

Facebook: **facebook.com/accofinaDotCom**

Twitter: **@accofina**

Google+: **https://plus.google.com/+accofina**

Amazon Review Request:

Also, it would be great to get an Amazon Review from you if you enjoyed, and got value, from this book.

Positive Amazon Reviews are worth their weight gold in the Amazon World and could possibly propel the little business, accofina, beyond its wildest expectations.

If you did get a positive experience from this book, it would be deeply appreciated if you could spare a couple of minutes to Rate the Book (on the final page of this eBook or on its Amazon product page) and maybe leave a positive Comment.

Thanks again.

www.ingramcontent.com/pod-product-compliance
Lightning Source LLC
Chambersburg PA
CBHW021436170526
45164CB00001B/264